Sing, O Daughter of Zion; shout aloud, O Israel! Be glad and rejoice with all your heart, O Daughter of Jerusalem! . . . "The LORD your God is with you, he is mighty to save. He will take great delight in you, he will quiet you with his love, he will rejoice over you with singing."

Zephaniah 3:14,17

believe that we were made for joy, but we have forgotten what it smells like. We've forgotten what it looks like. We've forgotten how it sounds. I think of the little girl who sneaked into her baby sister's room and whispered, "Tell me about God. I'm forgetting."

Sheila Walsh

When a sudden ray of sun or a moonbeam falls on a dreary street, it makes no difference what it illumines—a broken bottle on the ground, a fading flower in a field, or the flaxen blonde hair of a child's head. The object is transformed and the viewer is transfixed. Celebrate that moment of beauty and take it with you in your memory. It is God's gift to you.

Luci Swindoll

Laughter is a riotous vote of acceptance that God is the God-who-sees. Whatever it is probably won't go away, so we might as well live and laugh through it. When we double over laughing, we're bending so we won't break. If you think your particular troubles are too heavy and too traumatic to laugh about, remember that laughing is like changing a baby's diaper. It doesn't solve any problems permanently, but it makes things more acceptable for awhile.

Barbara Johnson

*T*hanks be to God, who always leads us in triumphal procession in Christ and through us spreads everywhere the fragrance of the knowledge of him.

2 Corinthians 2:14

The issue of cleanliness on this polluted planet is a constant one. Every day we shower, scrub, scrape, soak, and scour in an attempt to stay healthy and socially acceptable. In fact, I have a basket at my tubside filled with cleaning utensils: sponges, brushes, pumice, and soaps. As helpful as these items are, they do not compare to how clean I feel when I have spent moments in the Lord's presence. I am cleansed in the innermost parts of my being where even the sauna's steam can't penetrate.

Patsy Clairmont

Years ago a friend of mine offered to share her daylilies with me. I observed there were whole stalks of buds and that God's plan was that when one conked out—finished for the day—another one (or two) would open up. I pondered the thought that God felt it was worth it to create one flower to bloom for one day. If a lily is worth it, I'm worth it! That thought empowered me to go on when it would have been easy to give up.

Sue Buchanan

*I*f your love is for the left lane, swing on over there and feel the wind flying through your hair, and the bugs spatting against your dark glasses. But if the right lane beckons you, indulge your penchant for counting wildflowers in the field or discarded tennis shoes on the freeway. Most important, we must all remember, left-laners or right-laners, we are to be tender with each other.

Marilyn Meberg

e joyful at your Feast—you, your sons and daughters . . . For the LORD your God will bless you in all your harvest and in all the work of your hands, and your joy will be complete.

Deuteronomy 16:14–15

Lord, make me increasingly aware that to be chosen by You also includes Your choices of those who nurture me in ways too many and magnificent for me to imagine. The feast at which I am sitting is more luxurious than I can comprehend. My simple table blessing is inadequate, but . . . thank you!

Joy MacKenzie

From the moment I first held you in my arms, still drenched in birth, until now as I watch you drive away to the appointments you've made with life, mothering you has been my life's most joyful adventure. You baptized the common things with natal freshness and with the shower of your laughter. You gave me an excuse to be myself again, to skip down forest trails or sled the frozen hillsides, to splash through springtime puddles—bare-foot glad—and guess at where the shooting stars must go.

Gloria Gaither

If you're a parent, pain is inevitable, but misery is optional. As the saying goes, even the sun has a sinking spell every evening. But the next morning, like bread dough in the darkness of the oven, it rises. We Christian parents can hit bottom just like anyone else. But we have a special ability that nonbelievers don't have. We bounce! So when you feel yourself plummeting into the closet, be sure to leave the door open. That way you won't knock it down on your way out.

Barbara Johnson

The LORD is my strength and my shield;
my heart trusts in him, and I am
helped. My heart leaps for joy and I
will give thanks to him in song.

Psalm 28:7

Speaking of her son Christian:
Does he know that music has been a part of his world since before he was born? He's now eleven months old. He has a lot to say—so he sings. It serves him when he's so happy he could burst because he doesn't have the right words to say. We'll be standing in line at the grocery store and he'll burst into . . . something, at the top of his voice. Part of it seems to be his way of throwing out a cord—communication, shared joy.

Sheila Walsh

Gather up the gifts your friends have to offer—laughter, touching, listening, crying, good conversation, good casseroles, celebration—and put them in a big basket (figuratively speaking, of course). Use them as you need them, but for heaven's sake, don't expect everyone's gift to be the same!

Joy MacKenzie

I wonder what exclamation escaped Adam when he saw his first rhino, baboon, and ostrich. I bet if he had had a horn, he would have honked it all day. Or the series of oohs sung by Eve (which was probably the first aria) when she experienced a crimson sunset. And imagine the magnificent view the first couple must have had of the firmament without the distraction and diffusion of city lights and pollution.

Patsy Clairmont

Hallelujah! For the Lord God Almighty reigns. Let us rejoice and be glad and give him glory! For the wedding of the Lamb has come, and his bride has made herself ready.

Revelation 19:6–7

on't ever forget the place you have with Jesus. It is a place that is reserved for you and you alone—so close to his heart that on some days if you close your eyes and listen intently, you may hear his very breath. It is his breath that continually breathes life into your soul. You are so deeply loved. Walk arm in arm with him today. Your eternal escort. Your faithful bridegroom. He will never let you go.

Kathy Troccoli

I must admit the word *listening* has never been tops on my priority list of words. Somehow I have had the idea that talking was something you did while you thought about what you should be saying! My husband Bob used to say that I should learn to knit, so I would have something to think about while I talked.

Peggy Benson

What an incredible paradox I live in. To understand who I am without God and what I'm capable of without Jesus is so sobering. I'm easily subject to passions, lusts, lies, idols, sin, and death. At the same time, I know who I am in Jesus: a conqueror, a child of God, a sinner saved by grace, a receiver of the gift of heaven. I move in greater strength, growth, maturity, and grace when I keep this balancing truth in my heart and mind: "Wretched woman that I am, but beautiful bride of Christ."

Kathy Troccoli

You crown the year with your bounty, and your carts overflow with abundance. The grasslands of the desert overflow; the hills are clothed with gladness. The meadows are covered with flocks and the valleys are mantled with grain; they shout for joy and sing.

Psalm 65:11–13

A little child was walking one evening with his mother. He looked up at the sky and said, "Mommy, if the wrong side of heaven is this beautiful, imagine what the right side looks like!" Maybe we don't amount to much. But imagine how we'll look when we're turned right side out.

Barbara Johnson

Each day, each moment is so pregnant with eternity that if we "tune in" to it, we can hardly contain the joy. I have a feeling this is what happened to Moses when he saw the burning bush. Maybe Yahweh performed laser surgery on his eyes so he could see what was always there, and Moses was just so overwhelmed by the "glory" of God that the very ground he stood on became infused with "holiness" and the bushes along the mountain path burned with splendor.

Gloria Gaither

I was driving down a familiar road one fall day when I almost drove off the road, the beauty was so intense. It looked as if God had sent in a team of the world's finest artists overnight—and I was privy to the opening day of his spectacle. As I slowly drove along this festive row, leaves danced in the air and brushed against my windshield. It seemed as if I had landed in Oz. I was strongly tempted to get out and clap at God's imagination.

Sheila Walsh

To him who is able to keep you from falling and to present you before his glorious presence without fault and with great joy—to the only God our Savior be glory, majesty, power and authority, through Jesus Christ our Lord, before all ages, now and forevermore! Amen.

Jude 24–25

What about those of us who'd like to turn back the clock? Sure, we'd like to be younger and stronger again. More resilient. But remember Isaiah? He said to let the past lie. Look ahead. Someone has said, "Don't look back. You're not going that way." It is never too late to spend time on the important things. This minute is a gift. That's why we call it the present.

Barbara Johnson

Hugger-mugger looks and sounds like a made-up word, but it's not. It's an in-the-dictionary word that means "confusion; muddle; disordered"—in other words, one of life's tough times. My personal definition is, "I'm so confused I don't know from one minute to the next whether I'll be hugged or mugged." Prayer is the best way to help a friend through a tough time. Even secular research is discovering that prayer works. But of course, we knew it all along.

Sue Buchanan

As a child I pictured the true Christian as being a missionary. Here's what she looked like: Bangs cut extra short so that she wouldn't need another haircut for at least six months. The rest of her hair pulled so tightly in a bun that she looked permanently surprised (there would be no room for impure thoughts, as they were all strangled to death). A true Christian? Maybe not! We are made in the image of God, to be loving, faithful, true, compassionate, kind, creative, righteous, strong, tender, eternal.

Sheila Walsh

I will praise the LORD, who counsels me; even at night my heart instructs me. . . . You have made known to me the path of life; you will fill me with joy in your presence, with eternal pleasures at your right hand.

Psalm 16:7,11

I've noticed that, in the few moments of sleep you get when your children are babies, God mysteriously tucks love into your heart. You find your ocean of love is so deep it can carry you across the rough water of sleeplessness. Billy Sunday said, "Mothers fill places so great that there isn't an angel in heaven who wouldn't be glad to give a bushel of diamonds to come down here and take their place."

Sheila Walsh

Magic moments don't require special circumstances. You can tickle your kid when you tuck her into bed. You can kiss her toes and the tips of every finger. You can ask about her dearest wish when you're stirring the spaghetti or putting together a sack lunch. You can find her soft spots easier when she's very glad or very sad. Tap into who she is at those times when she's not busy proving herself to you and everybody else.

Barbara Johnson

When God said a joyful heart (or laughing heart) is good medicine, I believe he was literal in his meaning. The medical world has verified that laughter releases endorphins, God's natural painkillers, which are fifty to one hundred times more powerful than morphine. Don't you love that? The God of the universe has said all along that a joyful heart is good medicine. God has given us a prescription. All we have to do is fill the prescription.

Marilyn Meberg

*S*atisfy us in the morning with your unfailing love, that we may sing for joy and be glad all our days. . . . May the favor of the Lord our God rest upon us; establish the work of our hands.

Psalm 90:14,17

Friendship is a word full of growth potential. One can become bigger (as in character enlargement) or one can become smaller (as in narrow-minded). Becoming a good friend is aerobic in that it takes time and effort. When Jesus is our best friend, we won't approach human friendships from such a shallow place. When we turn to him first and then turn to others, we will be better prepared to give and receive relationally and rationally.

Patsy Clairmont

ored Royal Air Force pilots stationed on the Falkland Islands devised what they thought was a wonderful game. Noting that the local penguins seemed fascinated by airplanes, the pilots flew their planes slowly along the water's edge as nearly ten thousand penguins turned their heads in unison, watching the planes go by. To give the penguins a little variety, the pilots flew out to sea, turned around, and flew over the top of the penguin colony. Once again, in unison, heads went up, up, up, until all ten thousand penguins toppled softly onto their backs.

Marilyn Meberg

i continue to love recess. Wheee! I have learned along the journey how important play is to our lives as long as it is our minor and not our major. We were designed to work and to work heartily. I don't think there is any sweeter sleep than that which follows a diligent day's work. But without respite, work will wear us to a frazzle. Recess keeps the dazzle in our footwork.

Patsy Clairmont

The kingdom of heaven is like treasure hidden in a field. When a man found it, he hid it again, and then in his joy went and sold all he had and bought that field.

Matthew 13:44

Whatever your time, whatever your season, even in the midst of tragedy, there are moments worth savoring. Some of us have more sand on the bottom of our hourglass than at the top. (I'm not referring to our figures, even though they do tend to slip with the sand.) Yet, as long as breath is in our bodies, there will be moments, sweet moments, to revel in. This time is our time. Let's go savor the flavor!

Patsy Clairmont

My husband used to say, "In this life if you have two or three good friends, consider yourself fortunate." My friends are part of that *life* of my life that gives me warmth, color, texture, courage, comfort, strength, joy, tears, and very often, laughter. If I were asked what I cherish most, my answer would surely be my faith in God, but without so much as a comma between, I would have to add my exquisite treasure of friends and family. This is a collection I intend to keep.

Peggy Benson

Once a reporter stood in front of a fire as it consumed a house and then he turned to see the homeowners and their little son watching it burn. The reporter, fishing for a human interest angle, said to the boy, "Son, it looks as if you don't have a home anymore." The little boy promptly answered, "Oh, yes, we have a home. We just don't have a house to put it in."

Barbara Johnson

When I said, "My foot is slipping," your love, O LORD, supported me. When anxiety was great within me, your consolation brought joy to my soul. . . . The LORD has become my fortress, and my God the rock in whom I take refuge.

Psalm 94:18–19,22

When the hard times of life come, we know that no matter how tragic the circumstances seem, no matter how long the spiritual drought, no matter how long and dark the days, the sun is sure to break through; the dawn will come. The warmth of His assurance will hold us in an embrace once again, and we will know that our God has been there all along. We will hear him say, through it all, "Hold on, my child, joy comes in the morning!"

Gloria Gaither

Remember, a small trouble is like a pebble. Hold it too close to your eye and it puts everything out of focus. Hold it at proper viewing distance and it can be examined and classified. Throw it at your feet and see it in its true setting—just one more tiny bump on the pathway.

Barbara Johnson

Running to hide our faces in God is like seeking the comfort and familiarity of a childhood blanket that allows us to tune out the realities of our lives. God is a mighty lion, whose roar is heard in every corner of the world. Still, when you are in trouble, you can run to him and let him hide you in his mane.

Sheila Walsh

*D*o not lose heart. Though outwardly we are wasting away, yet inwardly we are being renewed day by day. For our light and momentary troubles are achieving for us an eternal glory that far outweighs them all.

2 Corinthians 4:16–17

More and more, I'm learning to embrace what life has to offer, to soak the poison out of it by taking in God's love in a way that helps me do, act, and say exactly what is in his heart to do, act, and say. And I only become a better woman for it. My heart continues to grow wider so that more of Jesus can dwell in me.

Kathy Troccoli

Instead of tapping or rapping, my way of dealing with the ever-present clock is flapping. I spread my stubby wings and try to lift my chubby frame off the ticking Tarmac only to crash-land like one of those gooney birds who flails beak first into the earth.

Patsy Clairmont

They say that once you're old enough to know all the answers, nobody asks you the questions anymore. But TV journalist Dan Rather once asked a 106-year-old man to disclose his secret of long life. The old man rocked back and forth in his chair before answering. Finally he replied, "Keep breathing."

Barbara Johnson

I will rejoice in the LORD, I will be joyful in God my Savior. The Sovereign LORD is my strength; he makes my feet like the feet of a deer, he enables me to go on the heights.

Habakkuk 3:18–19

My neighbor was cleaning out her garage when she found an old, damp, blue tarp. She decided to let it dry in the sun. A short time later she heard an unusual honking sound coming from her backyard. Mr. and Mrs. Daffy Duck had made a three-point landing beside the tarp, thinking it was a private pond. Alicia consoled the misguided pair as she pointed out that the tarp was not even a small puddle. (I think the featherbrains are still in therapy after that jolting revelation.)

Patsy Clairmont

The God of the universe has chosen you to know him! It's like crawling out of a ditch, covered in mud and debris, and being put on the best-dressed list. It's like being handed the Pulitzer Prize for literature when you can barely write your own name. It's like showing up with empty pockets at a benefit dinner for the needy and being voted benefactor of the year.

Sheila Walsh

A mother of two small children had become absorbed in reading while her three-year-old daughter and five-month-old son played quietly nearby. Suddenly the mother realized the children were no longer playing in the room. Panic-stricken, she went looking for them. She found them playing happily in her daughter's bedroom. Relieved and yet upset, she reminded her daughter, "You know you are not allowed to carry your little brother!" "I didn't, Mommy. I rolled him," the little girl said with a smile.

Barbara Johnson

Your light will break forth like the dawn, and your healing will quickly appear. . . . Then you will find your joy in the LORD, and he will cause you to ride on the heights of the land.

Isaiah 58:8,14

Think about your fears. How many of the feared disasters never actually came to pass, or if they did, how many of them really were more than you could handle? Mark Twain said, "I am an old man and have known a great many troubles, but most of them never happened." We waste a great deal of energy dreading devastation that often never happens.

Sheila Walsh

When from the ashes of bitter disappointment, new dreams rise like a phoenix on the strong wings of a new morning, and when we look back down the long road of our lives and see piles of ash like altars built along our path, we feel a simple chorus rising in our hearts: "Jesus is all that I need." He smiles at us—we know it—and whispers simply: "I am."

Gloria Gaither

Studies say that people who have friends live longer and have fewer illnesses, and that a close circle of friends actually helps the immune system work. With this in mind, run, don't walk, to your nearest neighborhood coffee klatch, church group, political club, or neighborhood bar. (Just kidding about the bar, but you get the drift!) You won't find that "close circle of friends" by sitting at home reading National Enquirer and watching TV! You do want your immune system to work, don't you?

Peggy Benson

*H*e has not left himself without testimony: He has shown kindness by giving you rain from heaven . . . he provides you with plenty of food and fills your hearts with joy.

Acts 14:17

If water is the most life-giving element on earth, then when rain comes we should all run out into it instead of running inside to get out of it. Instead of closing the windows and doors, we should fling them open to watch and hear and feel the life-sustaining gift being bestowed upon us all. We should gather our children and be bathed by the rain on our faces—and give thanks for the wonder of wonders.

Gloria Gaither

The spirit of the garden is the spirit of giving. It gives in all seasons. Even when it appears dead, deep in the heart of its soil, it is preparing to deliver once again in abundance and variety. We have friendships like that—friendships which, once nurtured, are now neglected. In the barren season, they go on giving. Where there is love, life renews itself with absolute certainty! Amazing!

Joy MacKenzie

I have discovered that my brain was not dead, only sleeping to avoid the chaos around me. And my soul, when watered, straightened right up like a refreshed plant. I may even bloom again. Who knows?

Gloria Gaither

nstead of their shame my people will receive a double portion, and instead of disgrace they will rejoice in their inheritance . . . and everlasting joy will be theirs.

Isaiah 61:7

have learned that uppity is a downer, for we are warned about being high-minded, that is, thinking more highly of ourselves than we should. Like the time I thought I was lookin' good only to discover my pantyhose were underfoot—or more accurately, they were streaming behind my foot as I sashayed through the middle of town. Not a pretty sight.

Patsy Clairmont

It takes courage to wear the symbols of Christianity. As soon as you slap a fish-shaped decal on your car, some turkey shows up at your door, saying he's just accidentally dumped a load of concrete all over your patio. It's much easier to wear a Christian symbol under your coat—or hide it under a bushel. Whether you wear a tiny, fish-shaped lapel pin or paint "Truckin' for Jesus" in letters two feet high on the side of your eighteen-wheeler, it's all the same to those who are watching.

Barbara Johnson

find that my best friends are those with whom the give-and-take is joyful and genuine—people with whom I can be myself, hiding neither warts nor marks of beauty, and with whom selflessness is never a chore. We are as happy for one another's successes as we are sad for failures. (Surprisingly, that's not easy for human beings!)

Gloria Gaither

Let the word of Christ dwell in you richly as you teach and admonish one another with all wisdom, and as you sing psalms, hymns and spiritual songs with gratitude in your hearts to God.

Colossians 3:16

Can't you tell when you're with someone who's listening? She hears you, really hears you. He hears the sadness in your tone or catches your joy. Be a listener, to music, to life, to others, to God. Life is noisy, but there is music in every heartbeat. God is waiting to bring joy and peace to the confusion of our days.

Sheila Walsh

riendship is not a machine—you can't just add more memory, more megabytes to make it better. If the joy is in the flow—the moments of great advance, the rush—then the maturing and growing is in the retreat, the pulling back, the ebb, during which there is a gradual preparation and anticipation of the next exciting surge forward.

Joy MacKenzie

I remember the day I picked up a card that showed Winnie the Pooh and Piglet on the front, walking hand in hand. Their conversation went like this:

"Pooh?" Piglet said.

"Yes, Piglet?"

"Oh, nothing," Piglet said. "I just wanted to be sure of you."

I've asked this question of close friends at different times in my life, in many different ways. I need the safety, the reassurance, the knowing that they are there and that I am loved.

Kathy Troccoli

you will go out in joy and be led forth in peace; the mountains and hills will burst into song before you, and all the trees of the field will clap their hands. Instead of the thornbush will grow the pine tree, and instead of briers the myrtle will grow.

Isaiah 55:12–13

Daffodils and tulips may be the first flowers to tenuously poke their impatient green noses out to test the spring temperatures, but those crusty crocuses are the real movers and shakers. With wild abandonment, they thrust their animated antennae into a frigid, unfriendly world and announce with cheerful exuberance, "Ready or not, here comes spring!"

Joy MacKenzie

My sister was ten years old when I was born, and I have never known life without her. In my heart I know the rarest thing we'll ever grow is the deep friendship that will never die with any season. Someone has said, "You can't take it with you," but I am convinced that what my sister and I have grown together is already being transplanted in the perfected Garden of Eden on the sunny banks of the Jordan.

Gloria Gaither

Sometimes life becomes so complicated we feel as if we've gone as far as we can down this stressful highway. We imagine ourselves smashed up against a brick wall, unable to answer one more call, hear one more complaint, and take one more breath. When that's the image that fills your mind, change the brick wall to God. Imagine yourself pressed tightly against his heart, wrapped in his everlasting arms, soothed by his life-giving breath. Picture yourself encircled in God's love, soaked in his strength.

Barbara Johnson

I will sing to the LORD, for he is highly exalted . . . . The LORD is my strength and my song; he has become my salvation . . . . In your unfailing love you will lead the people you have redeemed. In your strength you will guide them to your holy dwelling.

Exodus 15:1–2,13

i sang my final concert of 1996 two days before Christian was born. I felt like a show-and-tell exhibit as I sang of Mary's journey to Bethlehem. It was hard to catch my breath that evening, but I was doing fairly well until I came to "Silent Night," at which point Christian woke up in my womb and began to dance to the song. Have you ever tried to sing with a squirrel up your sweater?

Sheila Walsh

If it takes climbing windmills, marching in a parade, or ascending the down escalator to break out of your little, proper, plastic, grown-up mold, do it. Become a really dingy person—not din-gee but ding-ee. Even if people think you are fresh out of the rubber room.

Barbara Johnson

Some of my favorite concerts now take place in a white rocking chair in Christian's bedroom. He'll reach up and touch my face or lie back and listen. Sometimes he'll burst out laughing, which can be a little disconcerting if I'm halfway through "Jesus Loves Me." But he should laugh with delight. Martin Luther said, "The devil does not stay where music is."

Sheila Walsh

Rejoice in the Lord always. I will say it again: Rejoice! Let your gentleness be evident to all. The Lord is near. Do not be anxious about anything, but in everything, by prayer and petition, with thanksgiving, present your requests to God. And the peace of God, which transcends all understanding, will guard your hearts and your minds in Christ Jesus.

Philippians 4:4–7

Children teach us new levels of compassion. A young mother told me about her dismay when her little girl came home late from school one day. When she asked her daughter why she was so late, the little girl explained that her friend had dropped a china doll on the sidewalk, and it had broken into pieces. "So you stopped to help her fix the doll?" the mother asked. "No, Mommy. We knew we couldn't fix it, but I stopped to help her cry."

Barbara Johnson

At this point in my life the most difficult task that I attempt in any given day is to get clothes on my son. He wriggles. He moves at the wrong moment. Every now and then he'll lie back and bless his mother with the opportunity to clothe him without requiring oxygen at the end of it, and I count my blessings. So, too, we are called to relax in God and allow him to clothe us in his righteousness.

Sheila Walsh

Lily Tomlin says, "For fast-acting relief, try slowing down." Simply put, take a few minutes daily to ponder what is worthwhile about living. Stop whirling about like a pinwheel long enough to come to a rest and consider your next action. Just what is it you want to do? What do you need to do for the sake of your soul?

Luci Swindoll

The ransomed of the LORD will . . . enter Zion with singing; everlasting joy will crown their heads. Gladness and joy will overtake them, and sorrow and sighing will flee away.

Isaiah 35:10

L ife is a refining process. Our response to it determines whether we'll be ground down or polished up. On a piano, one person sits down and plays sonatas, while another merely bangs away at "Chopsticks." The piano is not responsible. It's how you touch the keys that makes the difference. It's how you play what life gives you that determines your joy and shine.

Barbara Johnson

have learned that it isn't necessary to resolve all differences for two people to be friends. I have learned that the space and air between two people are as important to a relationship as the times of unity and closeness. Life is a process and, to God, process is not a means to a goal. Process is the goal of life that keeps us moving closer, always closer to an intimate friendship with him.

Gloria Gaither

Road signs throughout the land alert us to many different animal crossings. Evidently once Noah parked the ark the creatures aboard hotfooted it down the plank and scattered in all directions. Man followed in close pursuit and poured roadways right across Silver, Eeyore, Bossie, and Bambi's pathways. This has caused some startling results as man and beast continue to meet head-on.

Patsy Clairmont

*D*o everything without complaining or arguing, so that you may become blameless and pure, children of God without fault in a crooked and depraved generation, in which you shine like stars in the universe as you hold out the word of life.

Philippians 2:14–16

You are God's kingdom star. You may be overweight, sport age spots, find a new crinkle in your face now and then. None of that matters. For your beauty is generated from the inside. Stars don't merely reflect the light of the sun like the moon does. Stars are little suns; they generate their own light.

Barbara Johnson

Theology is an interesting school of thought. The Bible is beautiful literature. Sitting in a quiet sanctuary, bathed in the amber light from stained-glass windows, having our jangled nerves soothed by the chords of the organ— all that is inspiring. But to tell you the truth, when we leave the classroom, close the church door, and walk out into the real world, it is the indisputable proof of changed lives that makes us believers.

Gloria Gaither

Watch out! God is making you authentic. Real. Rubbing off your fake fur. Changing your outlook. Giving you new desires. Making you marvelous. Fulfilling what you were created for. He is making you the "Queen of Quite a Lot," enlightening you for kingdom work. Open your arms wide to God's imaginative work in you. Be brave. Then braver still. Never resist His insistence on your perfection.

Barbara Johnson

*et all who take refuge in you be glad;
let them ever sing for joy. Spread your
protection over them, that those who
love your name may rejoice in you.*

Psalm 5:11

I believe that God is in our everyday no matter whether we see him, feel him, or hear him. Many moments occur in our lives which reveal his face, his touch, his voice. Look for him today. He will be found. You will be sweetly surprised at the many ways he surrounds you with his love.

Kathy Troccoli

Some of the "stuff" of life is mundane and draining while other parts of life are enormous and hard. Whatever the size of the difficulty, cheer is waiting to be discovered—sometimes unexpectedly, like a chocolate chip in the raisin bran.

Marilyn Meberg

A friend of mine claims we need bumpers—angel bumpers—on our cars to protect us from serious damage. My friend also suggests we equip ourselves with the shock absorber of laughter to make the journey easier and the windshield wipers of God's love to swish away the what-ifs so we can more clearly see what is.

Barbara Johnson

Because of his great love for us, God, who is rich in mercy, made us alive with Christ even when we were dead in transgressions—it is by grace you have been saved. And God raised us up with Christ and seated us with him in the heavenly realms in Christ Jesus, in order that in the coming ages he might show the incomparable riches of his grace, expressed in his kindness to us in Christ Jesus.

Ephesians 2:4–7

Time seems either to be in my face or to catapult by me. It can be as elusive as my income or as contrary as my weight. I don't necessarily want to harness time, but I'd like at least to corral it. One day, one glorious day, we will hear the wake-up call of all wake-up calls. We will be unencumbered with time limits, and instead of savoring a memory or a moment, we will savor the Savior . . . forever.

Patsy Clairmont

A thin line separates laughter and pain, comedy and tragedy, humor and hurt. Our lives constantly walk that line. When we slip off on one side or the other, we're taken by surprise. But who said there wouldn't be surprises? Knowing God just means that all the rules will be fair; at the end of our life drama, we'll see that.

Barbara Johnson

How do you change the habits of a lifetime? I love the line of Mark Twain: "You can't break a bad habit by throwing it out the window. You've got to walk it slowly down the stairs." Slowly and deliberately. Walking takes commitment. It takes the first step and the next and the next until you get to the door.

Sheila Walsh

Shout for joy to the LORD, all the earth. Worship the LORD with gladness; come before him with joyful songs. . . . Enter his gates with thanksgiving and his courts with praise; give thanks to him and praise his name. For the LORD is good and his love endures forever; his faithfulness continues through all generations.

Psalm 100:1–2,4–5

Every day is a Happy-Mother's-Day for the children of moms who are elastic, who can stretch. Who but a mother puts up with cranky toddlers or irritable teenagers free of charge? Who else gets up to make her own breakfast on her birthday? Who changes the empty toilet paper rolls? Never tires of inquiring, "Did you flush?" Lies awake on Saturday nights listening for the last chick to return to the nest? Who gathers all her eggs, puts them all in one basket, and then gives it to God?

Barbara Johnson

Since I've become a mother, I have a new appreciation for my own mom. When I realized what labor pains were all about, I wanted to buy her a small country! I now know, in such a deeper way, that the parent and the child are irrevocably part of the tapestry of each other's lives.

Sheila Walsh

When my grandson Ian had spoken the word "happy" in my presence, I was curious to know if he associated the word with an object or whether it had personal meaning for him. I assumed neither because, after all, he was only fourteen months old. But when he said "happy" within the meaningful context of yielding to his mama's comfort, he confirmed my deeply held convictions: The child is a genius. I must make phone calls.

Marilyn Meberg

have learned the secret of being content in any and every situation, whether well fed or hungry, whether living in plenty or in want. I can do everything through him who gives me strength.

Philippians 4:12–13

My darling daughter-in-love, Shannon, says life is like a dot-to-dot picture. When you begin, you have no idea what your life is going to turn out to be, she says. You start at one dot, and then another dot appears, and you jump off the first dot to land on the next one, hoping for the best. Sometimes a dot can be a huge, black hole. Occasionally, dots are tear-shaped. On others you feel like dancing—maybe those are the polka dots!

Barbara Johnson

Computers are utterly inexplicable to me. Not only that, but they also have an attitude. For instance, something as simple as shutting down the computer sends the little demonic person who scowlingly sits inside the machine day and night into parental mode. A question flashes on the screen: "Are you sure you want to shut down your machine?" Until the question was asked, I was quite certain I wanted to shut it down, but with those bold words glaring at me, I hesitate. Does the little person know something I don't?

Marilyn Meberg

Someone once said, "I used to take each day as it came, one at a time. Now I'm down to a half day at a time!" Growing older is sometimes like climbing a steep hill. You can complain, "Too many rocks in the way and bumps on the road!" Or you can look at it this way, "I'd like to live my life in the fast lane, but I'm married to a speed bump." But the most productive way is to put your intellect and spirit to work doing what you do best.

Barbara Johnson

How beautiful on the mountains are the feet of those who bring good news, who proclaim peace, who bring good tidings, who proclaim salvation, who say to Zion, "Your God reigns!"

Isaiah 52:7

A mother in Bartonville, Illinois, tells the story of her daughter who was busy painting a portrait that she claimed was of God. When the mother pointed out that nobody knew what God looked like, the child said, "They will when I'm finished."

Luci Swindoll

One of my favorite early spring flowers is the johnny jump-up. They have sweet smiling faces, each with its own personality. They remind me that I have some wonderful jump-up friends in my life—people who have come into my life over the years at just the exact time I needed to see a friendly, smiling face.

Peggy Benson

You never know how God is working through your prayers or how He is using what you try to do, even when you don't see results. Live motherhood to the hilt. Bequeath your kisses and your discipline generously. Raise the standard of faith along with a finger to scold or correct. Spread your arms wide to a kid with a skinned knee. Lift a chin, hold a hand, tickle a foot. Keep the good times glowing. Make sure praise is flowing. You are a mother. Be glad!

Barbara Johnson

*J*esus said to me, "My grace is sufficient for you, for my power is made perfect in weakness." . . . That is why, for Christ's sake, I delight in weaknesses, in insults, in hardships, in persecutions, in difficulties. For when I am weak, then I am strong.

2 Corinthians 12:9,10

riendship is perhaps the most vulnerable of our cherished relationships. Unlike the unions of marriage and family its only ties are of the heart. And the stronger our need for a friend, the more tenacious our grip. But close observation of lasting friendships reveals people who are able to allow others to come and go in and out of the days of their lives with ease and grace. No grand entrances or notable exits; they simply pick up where they left off!

Joy MacKenzie

I've noticed that some folks have ducklike qualities: indecisive, looking for a handout, residuers, misguided, and on the verge of quacking up. Oh, my, I think I've just described my menopausal self. Since entering estrogen poverty I haven't been sashaying through life as I once did. I now have trouble with major decisions: Should I brush my teeth first or wash my face? These mental stumbling blocks can slow down one's day, not to mention one's productivity.

Patsy Clairmont

We cannot always head off disaster. Sometimes we discover that the light at the end of the tunnel really is the headlight of an oncoming train. Even so, Satan will not get the victory. Christian women will keep on risking their hearts whatever happens.

Barbara Johnson

*S*hout for joy, O heavens; rejoice, O
earth; burst into song, O mountains!
For the LORD comforts his people and
will have compassion on his afflicted ones.

Isaiah 49:13

A laugh lifestyle is predicated upon our attitude toward the daily stuff of life. When those tasks seem too dull to endure, figure out a way to make them fun; get creative and entertain yourself. If the stuff of life for you right now is not dull and boring but instead painful and overwhelming, find something in the midst of the pain that makes you smile and giggle anyway. There's always something somewhere even if you have to just pretend to laugh until you really do.

Marilyn Meberg

Some days "thank you" may seem to be a head-in-the-sand platitude offered out of compulsion rather than authenticity. But I believe it's the most authentic thing we can say. I believe that because of who it is we are thanking. We are not asking to stake our life savings on a broken down three-legged horse whose heart may see the finish line but whose body never will. This is God we are talking about! The great and good I AM.

Sheila Walsh

i love the sea. I love the certainty and the uncertainty of it, its amazing power and its sweet gentleness. It reminds me that a God who can be explained by the mind is no God at all, but an idol constructed by my own hands or, worse, a house pet on a leash. I must stand beside the ocean often so that I will not forget that. I must never create God in my image. His ways are immeasurably higher than my ways.

Gloria Gaither

As the Father has loved me, so have I loved you. Now remain in my love. If you obey my commands, you will remain in my love. . . . I have told you this so that my joy may be in you and that your joy may be complete.

John 15:9–11

I fling joy—beyond my next-door neighbor's fence, clear across town, and into the universe. Then it curves right back to me. Sometimes with a whack on the head when I need it. Sometimes with a thwack into my heart. Sometimes landing with a crack at my feet. But it always comes back. No doubt about it.

Barbara Johnson

All my life, my very favorite human invention has been the alphabet: twenty-six little soldiers ready to do battle at my command. They are lined up there, neatly, in alphabetical order, and when they are called out in squadrons, think of what they can do. Alone, these individual units are all but meaningless, but when they come together they can change the course of history. And that's often the way we are as people. We need each other. Two are better than one.

Luci Swindoll

How can I start a new year without attention to silence and an inward journey into space—the space within myself, the space without? It is space that traces around me, like a child traces around her hand on a clean page of paper, separating what is me from the throng of other souls on this crowded earth. Without the space, I would blend into the masses and, in time, forget that I am.

Gloria Gaither

The desert and the parched land will be glad; the wilderness will rejoice and blossom. Like the crocus, it will burst into bloom; it will rejoice greatly and shout for joy.

Isaiah 35:1–2

have never been one to rush around. One reason I love being Texan by birth is that we're well known for our two speeds: slow . . . and stop. We have lived by an inner rule of thumb that says, "I ain't goin' nowhere because this is the place to be. If I stay here, I don't have to hurry." I'd rather be at an airport an hour before my departure time, just so I don't have to hustle my bustle. And my very favorite exercise is a brisk sit.

Luci Swindoll

Leroy Walker was a turtle who had been tyrannizing Mrs. Boden's garden. In desperation one evening, she walked across the street and asked if I at age five would like to have this turtle for my very own. Getting permission from my parents, I eagerly took on the task of corralling Leroy. I had visions of great, companionable walks, my turtle and I. I managed to tie a string around his neck. The unhappy result was that he clunked along the sidewalk, legs and head ensconced in his shell. Our bonding activities were severely limited.

Marilyn Meberg

The famous American architect, Frank Lloyd Wright, believed the natural contours of the earth should blend inherently with man-made structures. "No house should ever be on any hill," he said. "It should be of the hill, belonging to it, so hill and house could live together each the happier for the other." Beauty is not just in the countenance of something. Beauty is in the physiognomy—in the expression and character of what makes up the beauty.

Luci Swindoll

Praise be to the God and Father of our Lord Jesus Christ! In his great mercy he has given us new birth into a living hope through the resurrection of Jesus Christ from the dead, and into an inheritance that can never perish, spoil or fade—kept in heaven for you.

1 Peter 1:3–4

Someone once said that life is made up of the tender teens, the teachable twenties, the tireless thirties, the fiery forties, the fretful fifties, the serious sixties, the sacred seventies, the aching eighties . . . shortening breath, death, sod, God. That is our journey, and a happy ending awaits us after we make our way through all the tough stuff.

Barbara Johnson

Looking for the essence of beauty is comprehending and appreciating that quality in an object which is fairer and better than only what our eyes see or our ears hear—whether that be a patch of blue in an overcast sky, the fleeting laughter from a voice we love, or something as unexpected as the rainbow colors in a spot of oil on the driveway.

Luci Swindoll

There is no situation in this life that God will not miraculously lead us through— giving us a strength and peace that we know is beyond anything we could conjure up. Lean on him. Abandon yourself to his grace. God will give you strength when you need it.

Kathy Troccoli

The people walking in darkness have seen a great light; on those living in the land of the shadow of death a light has dawned. You have enlarged the nation and increased their joy.

Isaiah 9:2–3

I loved reading Erma Bombeck. She was right up my alley, laughing over things I could relate to, like this: "One exercise program has you doing entire routines while cleaning house. It sounded so simple to bend over my vacuum cleaner and extend my right leg straight behind me while I touched my head to my knee. That was just before the vacuum sucked up my nightgown, causing me to nearly pass out!"

Barbara Johnson

In pursuit of a relationship with Jesus, we are being changed into his likeness. At that point, all the bewildering questions may remain unanswered. But—as the old-timers used to say—we are finding we don't have such a gnawing need to know the answers when we know the Answer. We are coming, as the poet Rilke said, to love the question and get more comfortable with the paradox of God. When we trust the author, we don't have to know the story. We just know it will be true.

Gloria Gaither

Our capacity to feel, to think, and to experience is so great—to taste the sweetness of joy that life can bring, to bask in the peace of God, to worship on the mountaintops, to ride high on loving and being loved. All of these are wonderful and precious gifts, and I'm so thankful for them as I journey through this earthly life.

Kathy Troccoli

*N*ow to him who is able to do immeasurably more than all we ask or imagine, according to his power that is at work within us, to him be glory in the church and in Christ Jesus throughout all generations, for ever and ever! Amen.

Ephesians 3:20–21

In moments that appear unredeemable, watch and wait. Recognize the precious things. Refuse to trash anything! Ask God to help you see things from His perspective. Take one step after another. Before long, in spite of yourself, you may notice surprising signs of hope in your own backyard: the chuckle of a baby, the kindly light in a neighbor's eyes, the sweet kiss of a spouse, an undreamed of opportunity.

Barbara Johnson

The freeway is the last place we think of slowing down or savoring our present moment. We simply want to get the driving over with, so we tear along with all our gripes and derring-do and madness, sometimes risking our very lives. Whether you're battling traffic with danger and risks on all sides, or sitting in your rocking chair knitting a sweater for your granddaughter, remember to be all there. Wherever you are now is God's provision, not his punishment.

Luci Swindoll

When I bought some new makeup recently, the salesgirl told me that if I dropped a little BB in the bottle and shook it before each use, the makeup wouldn't get thick and gooey. A day or so later, my husband Bill came in smiling broadly and gave me a huge plastic carton. Inside were 10,000—that's ten thousand!—BBs. God has given us a good measure, pressed down, shaken together, and running over. But most of the time, we need only one BB.

Barbara Johnson

Sing to the LORD a new song, for he has done marvelous things. . . . Shout for joy to the LORD, all the earth, burst into jubilant song with music. . . . Let the rivers clap their hands, let the mountains sing together for joy.

Psalm 98:1,4,8

As long as we're talking computer absurdities, can anyone tell me why on earth the pointer is called a mouse? For goodness sake, a mouse is a rodent! I can't imagine anything more repellent than having daily hand contact with something called a mouse. If we have to have an image of something small and furry that illogically represents a pointer, why not call it a canary?

Marilyn Meberg

Did you know researchers say that the simple act of turning your lips up (instead of down) stimulates good feelings? No matter how down you feel, how rotten, try smiling at yourself in every mirror you pass. First thing in the morning. Last thing at night. Broaden those luscious lips. Twist them toward heaven. You'll feel perkier faster if you smile than you would if you wallowed in gloomy thoughts.

Barbara Johnson

I need friends the way I need to garden. I need the challenge of it—preparing the soil, working at the task. Blooms don't just happen, you know! I need the cultivation process—giving it time and attention, learning when to water, when to feed, and when to be patient. Finally, I need to see the color of the garden—the rewards of a job well done. It's in the beauty and the bounty that we see the results of our efforts.

Peggy Benson

Though you have not seen Jesus, you love him; and even though you do not see him now, you believe in him and are filled with an inexpressible and glorious joy, for you are receiving the goal of your faith, the salvation of your souls.

1 Peter 1:8–9

We're all gardeners of the heart. Gardeners—because some ancient longing is built into us for the good, sweet earth. There is something evocative about the setting where Adam first met Eve. These two lovers walked with their Creator in the still of the evening as the Lord hit heaven's dimmer switch. There, at twilight, among the scent of roses and jasmine and apple blossoms, they savored a fellowship we can only dream about.

Barbara Johnson

saw a good one several years ago when I was standing at a public counter in a nearby city hall. It was typed on a small card and taped to the wall: "If you don't believe in the resurrection of the dead, stick around here till 5 p.m."

Luci Swindoll

I heard a story about a mother of four teenage daughters, about the same size as she. To keep her own laundry from disappearing into their drawers by mistake, this mother started marking her underwear "MOM." Finding her dresser drawer empty one morning, she went straight to the girls. "Do any of you have underwear that says 'MOM' on it?" she asked. One daughter spoke up quickly. "No, all of mine say 'WOW'!"

Barbara Johnson

Speak to one another with psalms, hymns and spiritual songs. Sing and make music in your heart to the Lord, always giving thanks to God the Father for everything, in the name of our Lord Jesus Christ.

Ephesians 5:19–20

Learning to be thrifty has always been a challenge for me. I'm a "more the merrier" kind of gal. Although, I have noticed, the more I ramble the more I gamble. There's such a thin line between having said just enough and having said way too much.

Patsy Clairmont

Mark Twain once said, "Everyone should have at least two friends—one who sees eye to eye about everything—another who disagrees about nearly everything." I have always thought a lovelier notion is that everyone should have a friend whom one can trust with both responses—comfortably!

Joy MacKenzie

Our church is divided into small fellowship groups that meet at various times during the week. Ours meets every Sunday evening and I can assure you we're faithful to Scripture. You know the verse—the one that says, "Where two or three are gathered in My name, someone will bring a casserole!"

Sue Buchanan

ear friends, do not be surprised at the painful trial you are suffering, as though something strange were happening to you. But rejoice that you participate in the sufferings of Christ, so that you may be overjoyed when his glory is revealed.

1 Peter 4:12–13

Through the maze and amazement of many years of relationships, I have learned that all friends aren't meant to be for a lifetime. In the garden of friendship, too, there are annuals and perennials. Some demand careful tending while others flourish with little attention. It helps to remember that though human relationships, like flowers, require human intervention, a Sovereign Master Gardener is in charge. He plans not only the original mix of genus, color, height, fullness, and durability, but he knows exactly in what space at what time each can bloom to its full potential.

Gloria Gaither

The need to post Private Road signs in my life has increased with the years. I need restorative times. My need for rest has multiplied into sporadic nap-ettes. Those in my audience are often thrown by my sometimes laid-back demeanor offstage; I go from Tigger onstage to Eeyore offstage. Learning to live with my limitations and to separate myself at times from people is difficult but imperative. And even though I may resist doing it, afterward I experience a rapid return of strength, and I'm able to maintain my joy.

Patsy Clairmont

Whatever your troubles, try looking at them by the light of another source or a different star. Go ahead; don't be afraid. Find a wacky angle, a new twist. Don't offer trouble the energy you should be using to train your boomerang arm. Offer trouble a little serious thought, then turn it upside down and look at it through God-colored glasses. Chew on trouble's possibilities for making you smarter, better, stronger, kinder. Then take the curved weapon I call joy and toss trouble by its funny side out into the world.

Barbara Johnson

ou are a chosen people, a royal priesthood, a holy nation, a people belonging to God, that you may declare the praises of him who called you out of darkness into his wonderful light.

1 Peter 2:9

have consciously sought after those things which make for value, order, richness, spirit and wonder, even though I am often unable to verbalize what I feel when I perceive something beautiful. Sometimes it's a pang or a sensation; at other times it is an awareness of joy and security or pure pleasure. In any event, it is a moment to be celebrated. Beauty justifies itself. The fact that it is beyond definition means nothing.

Luci Swindoll

Calvin, a bachelor, decided to buy a parrot. The parrot had been settled in his cage for only a few moments when a stream of loud oaths began to pour forth from the bird's beak. During one especially offensive cursing episode, Calvin flung it in the freezer and slammed the door. Calvin waited a few minutes before cautiously opening the freezer door. To his surprise, the parrot stood there looking back at him. "Sir," the parrot faltered, glancing around him at the contents of the freezer, "would you mind telling me what the chicken did?"

Marilyn Meberg

Next time you think you hear nothing in response to your prayers, don't assume God isn't listening. He may simply want you to rest in his shadow until he reveals his answer. When you hear a direct no, remind yourself there will always be a better yes. God is for you, and he will work out everything in conformity with the purpose of his will.

Kathy Troccoli

Sources

Friends Through Thick and Thin (Grand Rapids, MI: Zondervan Publishing House, 1998).

Joy Breaks (Grand Rapids, MI: Zondervan Publishing House, 1997).

Gloria Gaither, *Because He Lives* (Grand Rapids, MI: Zondervan Publishing House, 1997).

Barbara Johnson, *Boomerang Joy* (Grand Rapids, MI: Zondervan Publishing House, 1998).

Barbara Johnson, *The Joy Journal* (Dallas, TX: Word, 1996).

Marilyn Meberg, *I'd Rather Be Laughing* (Dallas, TX: Word, 1998).

Luci Swindoll, *You Bring the Confetti* (Dallas, TX: Word, 1997).

The Joyful Journey (Grand Rapids, MI: Zondervan Publishing House, 1997).

Kathy Troccoli, *My Life Is In Your Hands* (Grand Rapids, MI: Zondervan Publishing House, 1997).

Sheila Walsh, *Bring Back the Joy* (Grand Rapids, MI: Zondervan Publishing House, 1998).

Sheila Walsh, *Honestly* (Grand Rapids, MI: Zondervan Publishing House, 1997).

We Brake for Joy! (Grand Rapids, MI: Zondervan Publishing House, 1998).